The Book of Blue

by

Rebecca Anne Banks

Tea at Tympani Lane Records

www.tympanilanerecords.com

Order this book online at www.trafford.com
or email orders@trafford.com

Most Trafford titles are also available at major online book retailers.

Printed in the United States of America.

ISBN: 978-1-4669-9362-4 (sc)
ISBN: 978-1-4669-9363-1 (e)

Trafford rev. 05/20/2013

 www.trafford.com

North America & international
toll-free: 1 888 232 4444 (USA & Canada)
phone: 250 383 6864 ♦ fax: 812 355 4082

" For Blue,

    above the trees

    a piece of my sky,

    you'll always be a piece of my heart

    Blue,

    you are the dove. "

The First Book of Blue

Written the night of August 6th, 2011.

B lue,
you are the dove.

S o nice to see you
by my backdoor

my blue cloud

I tried to reconcile

the evening to the sky

the blue

and the disconnect

the reckoning of rain

and you so quiet

in the silence . . .

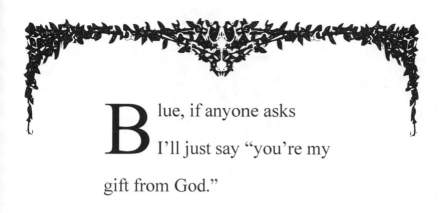

B lue, if anyone asks
I'll just say "you're my
gift from God."

I hold you
in the hollow space

in my gut

watch you in doorways,

Blue

watch the sky,

pray for rain.

B lue,
they made you a soldier

without meaning to

threw up the board

pinned you

made you wander

through the flower garden,

took away your home . . .

O' Blue
you wander in

in some quiet haze

I'm never quite certain

what pulls you here

but I am always

glad to see you.

B lue,
I sing to you

all my quiet songs

I write to you

all my quiet verse

I dance for you, quiet

under the blue, blue sky . . .

Under the blue night sky
you sleep

so quiet

I imagine rain

but I think you

dance

with the wind and the trees,

in your dreams.

O' Blue

you sit on my velvet chair

like a rain cloud

quiet

roll around the place

like an unmade bed,

you need to sleep

and disappear,

quiet.

B lue,
when you leave

I'm never quite certain

if I will see you again

the too much high

the too much low

we are friends of the sky.

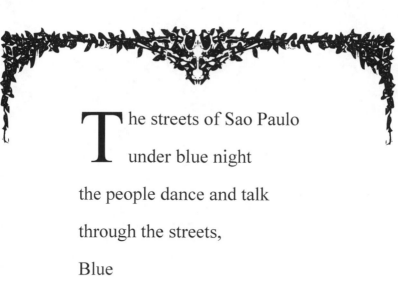

The streets of Sao Paulo

under blue night

the people dance and talk

through the streets,

Blue

I wander the dark . . .

I miss you.

B lue,
you are the dove.

The Second Book of Blue

B lue,
you are the dove.

T he night is quiet
Blue,

sometimes you'd be feeling good

and we'd talk and talk

sometimes there never seemed

anything left to say, quiet

tonight, like most nights

I pray for you,

out somewhere, under the sky.

I could remember the night of rain
Blue,

the soft light

as if you were here

in the quiet,

out of the rain . . .

T his evening, the sky is so beautiful,
　Blue

light jewels through the trees

the kettle is on the stove

the steady hum, fills the quiet . . .

into night.

B lue, I sing for you
a bird in the night

waiting for daylight,

by windows on the sky.

Y ou are my Thursday gift
     I love your warmth

your quiet

Blue

you come by

and then

go quickly

go quiet . . .

I feel your warmth

even after you have gone.

Quiet, he comes on the evening

beautiful Blue

as if expected skies

he gives me a gift

before I can talk

he is gone,

quiet, as if expected skies.

The butterfly tree

swarming oranges

down in Mexico

by blue sky,

the dance of free and home.

H e is kissed by the open road
held by God and the sky

Blue

so free

some lost child, found.

The August wind and rain

stirs the trees

makes them dance

on the last warm of Summer

the quiet immolation of light

white on sky

misplaced pieces of a quilt

in blue rhyme.

Quiet, the wind

blowing on the stars

brings you to me

Blue, lost in the day

so quiet . . .

B lue,
you are the dove.

The Third Book of Blue

B lue,
you are the dove.

I could hear
the hollow clang of bells

on Summer morning

the red of roses

the last of rain

Blue, the quiet of time

as if I could hold you,

quiet, against the sky.

As if kissed
by shadows of the rain

Blue, song and dance

I long to gather you in,

a place, inside the sky.

I read my poems
as if I am holding you,

Blue

it is night

as you hold me in the quiet . . .

U nder the skies of autumn
the night is cold, silent

Blue,

thoughts that ring as if spoken

a place struck in stone,

without you.

O' Blue

O' my soul . . .

If I wait by the gate

someone will come

the clouded sky

hangs dark

holds its breath

the quiet

Blue,

flower of Summer

sleeps . . .

The world is quiet
Blue

quiet place

I sing for you . . .

I could kiss your hands
sweet

as if the last of sunlight

upon roses

O' sweet night

Blue,

that sings . . .

Subterranean blue

under the sky of night

sweet growth

forest island

sing so sweet . . .

Blue copper welt sky
quiet darkening

to the ground

longs for the kiss

of sun

light and heat

blue, blue against the sky.

You run
    through my hands

like constant memory

Blue,

water on stone.

B^{lue,}
you are the dove.

The Fourth Book of Blue

B
lue,
you are the dove.

B lue, any peace
you may find

in trees

so quiet

against the sky.

He sits
so comfortably

on a pile of stones

Blue

the road

and sky

your home . . .

The Spirit blows
so big the wind

quiet, out over us

Blue, some big love song

under the moon.

O' sweet sky, Blue
some gentle talk,
you leave my hands full.

Windsong leaves
and rain

the quiet

Blue,

you haunt the edges of the sky.

H e is blown on light
and Blue

the winds of autumn,

darkening sky.

S ome expected child
I kiss your wrist

hold you,

close as the Autumn rain.

The china blue black sky
quiet prayers

to the Spirit,

Blue,

quiet . . .

He is of the sky

the quiet

that sings

Blue,

so sweet

into night.

S unlight and roses
the days

by blue sky

the nights

by song

and Blue . . .

Sweet the tree

and singing bird,

songs of night.

A bandoned to the trees
and sky

the dance of found

and Blue

wandering,

at the feet of the Father

je soif.

A roaming he does go.

B^{lue,}
you are the dove.

The Fifth Book of Blue

B lue,
you are the dove.

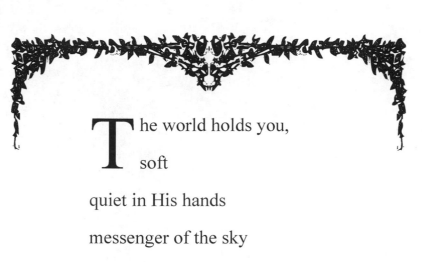

T he world holds you,
soft

quiet in His hands

messenger of the sky

quiet Blue,

I hold you soft

in quiet . . .

Within the night
the blue

in light

dances

casts against sweet

the rose,

soft

in quiet dark.

C old the night
sweet and bright

to find you sitting there

Blue

with apples and oranges

by the road,

some angel of glory and happenstance

who loves me

under autumn skies.

H e is of the Spirit
quiet,

in love and warm

some child of the night

touched by too much rain

and the sun

I would give you shelter,

Blue

my friend the sky knows.

Some wandering landscape
under the sky

we take off our clothes

in the Summer rain

Blue,

I hold you

you refuse to let me go

in some enchanted garden

at the end of night.

Spirits of the road
we haunt the places

of quiet

Blue

O' silent night

somewhere

under the shelter

of the sky.

L ost to the night
the sky holds him

sweet,

child of the Blue

and home.

Inside some museum piece
the turquoise leaf

on umber ground,

bright with orange fruit

and snails, quiet

Blue, this is how I think of you . . .

I sit in the palm of his hand
the flower

of the night

Blue, so sweet the rain

kisses the sky.

I kiss the palm of his hand

some sweet memory

of the sky

sweet song of Blue

the Spirit sings for you.

Sometimes the miles of time
you can feel it

under your feet

lost inside the night

blue and wandering

without . . .

O f an afternoon

the time of light

and warm Summer

as if the sky kissed

the earth

inside the blue

for hours

of an afternoon.

B^{lue,}
you are the dove.

The Sixth Book of Blue

B lue,
you are the dove.

The God of the flower.

That I could love

so well Summer

Blue, he that dances

with creations song . . .

S ome dream
I could fall into

the quiet remonstrations

of Blue

waves of forgetting . . .

somewhere I watch the light,

soft

dance across your face

in the peace of angels.

L ost in you
the quiet

Blue

the rose in a gun

somewhere

looking over my shoulder

past the cacophonies,

whispers in my head . . .

lost in you,

the quiet.

Unwritten cloth
I cry like a child

my hand on laces

bound, Blue

I open you like a gift

feed you chocolate

under Summer skies.

T he tamarind seed
no apologies for love,

Blue,

love letters in the rain,

news from a distance.

O utpost
some blue quiet

night

so beautiful

to hear from you

"I'll be home soon"

Q uiet talk
over morning coffee

you wake me beautiful,

Blue . . .

we walk in the warm

under gray skies, Autumn

sit outside

watch the day.

In the antiquarian Summer house
the terracotta floor

and the dressings of orange flowers

kissed by sunlight

a last look

and a hug

Blue, past the silence of winter.

As if attending
some delicate beauty

the love

of orange flowers,

Blue,

inside the winter.

Orange flower on table

some last look

of love

orange flowers

under sunlight,

Blue,

a gift from the night.

S now angels
imprints of love

Blue,

the winter

so sweet

by the playing

of the spoons . . .

B lue,
you are the dove.

The Seventh Book of Blue

B lue,
you are the dove.

I could paint you
with the day

the light and warm

of sun

so sweet the Summer,

so sweet

against you . . .

H e recreates the world
the new day

each time

he enters the room

Blue

and soul sweet

O' gentle Zen of Summer

he who lives

inside the sky.

Some beautiful storm
on a winter's day

Blue

after you go

I watch the sky

quiet . . .

Angel of the blue
and night

calling soft

calling sweet

against the cold

of morning . . .

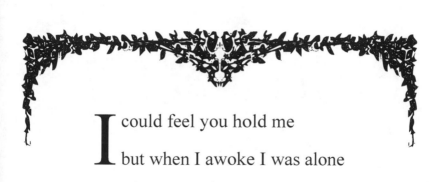

I could feel you hold me
but when I awoke I was alone

in the quiet

of Blue . . .

The Tahitian night

we dress for dinner

the heat and flowers

the dance of Blue

and full

the warm

against the sky.

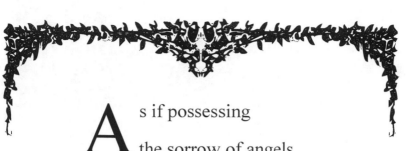

As if possessing

the sorrow of angels

and all the hope

in one place

my heart

is big with love, Blue

(the passion of found)

I can count
on so many hands

the times

I have longed to undress you

and worship, Blue

kiss you sweet

until the sky falls down.

I n this moment
the world is perfect

perfect Blue.

S o wild under the sky
Blue, I feed you . . .

B lue,
you are the dove . . .

The Eighth Book of Blue

B
lue,
you are the dove.

The street knows him
like a lover

Blue, he dances

under street lamps

lost child found.

T he quiet of my desiring
Blue, an angel

from the night . . .

quiets in

from the rain.

T hrough the broken window
such a beautiful heartache

Blue,

the love

not quite past

the dark of night

the fire

of flower

rests quiet,

sleeps against love.

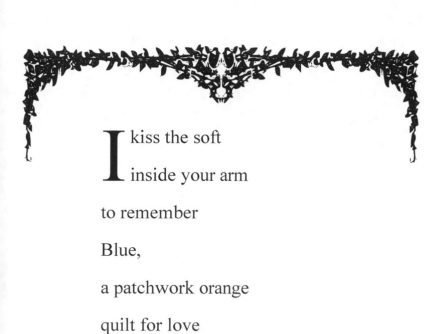

I kiss the soft
inside your arm

to remember

Blue,

a patchwork orange

quilt for love

and kisses quiet . . .

The man with the blue umbrella

gray sky day

we look for rain

have coffee

the dog dances

talk of "give me sunshine"

you plant roses in my heart

Blue, the man with the blue umbrella.

E ven in the rain
the tulips bloom

in warm

Summer dreams

quiet Blue.

S pirit dance
dance heart

Blue rhymes

with love.

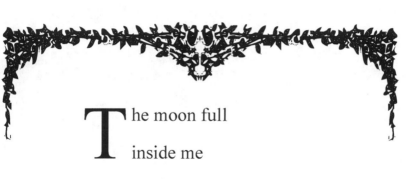

The moon full
inside me

blowing on Summer

Blue, nights

the heat wakes the sky

walks the day

into love.

Blue,
you are the dove.

The Ninth Book of Blue

B lue,
you are the dove.

Quiet in my hallway

Blue, the night

you stand, so quiet

wind blown Blue

some broken fall on

I talk in whispers

invite you in . . .

you slip down the stairs

a shadow

out into the night.

H e that dances with words
the light pours in

holds us,

gentles incantations

and sweet candy wine

sweet inside the Spirit

Blue,

warm into night.

S un and shadow
Summer days

quiet Blue

the sky holds the day still

without you.

B lue, so quiet the night
beside me

warm against winter.

Quiet outtakes

knit the heart

in the breath

of Summer.

Heart like a wheel

his song

of Summer

Blue . . .

it's the winter I remember

and the nights

into warm

you so quiet

beside me.

Blue, the one that holds me
sweet into light

and gold

hands cupped with flowers

run like water

falling to the ground

entwined in hearts

and whispers

warm,

under Summer skies.

The peace of the night

holds me, Blue

when you come close

a blanket

the quiet in warm . . .

As if going to an antique blue book
wiping the dust off

"yours forever"

and asleep . . .

B^{lue,}
you are the dove.